This book is written to provide information and motivation to readers. Its purpose is not to render any type of psychological, legal, or professional advice of any kind. The content is the sole opinion and expression of the author, and not necessarily that of the publisher.

Copyright © 2023 by Enrico Miguel Thomas.

All rights reserved. No part of this book may be reproduced, transmitted, or distributed in any form by any means, including, but not limited to, recording, photocopying, or taking screenshots of parts of the book, without prior written permission from the author or the publisher. Brief quotations for noncommercial purposes, such as book reviews, permitted by Fair Use of the U.S. Copyright Law, are allowed without written permissions, as long as such quotations do not cause damage to the book's commercial value. For permissions, write to the publisher, whose address is stated below.

Printed in the United States of America.

ISBN 978-1-64552-214-0 (Paperback)
ISBN 978-1-64552-205-8 (Digital)

Lettra Press books may be ordered through booksellers or by contacting:

Lettra Press LLC
30 N Gould St. Suite 4753
Sheridan, WY 82801
1 307-200-3414 | info@lettrapress.com
www.lettrapress.com

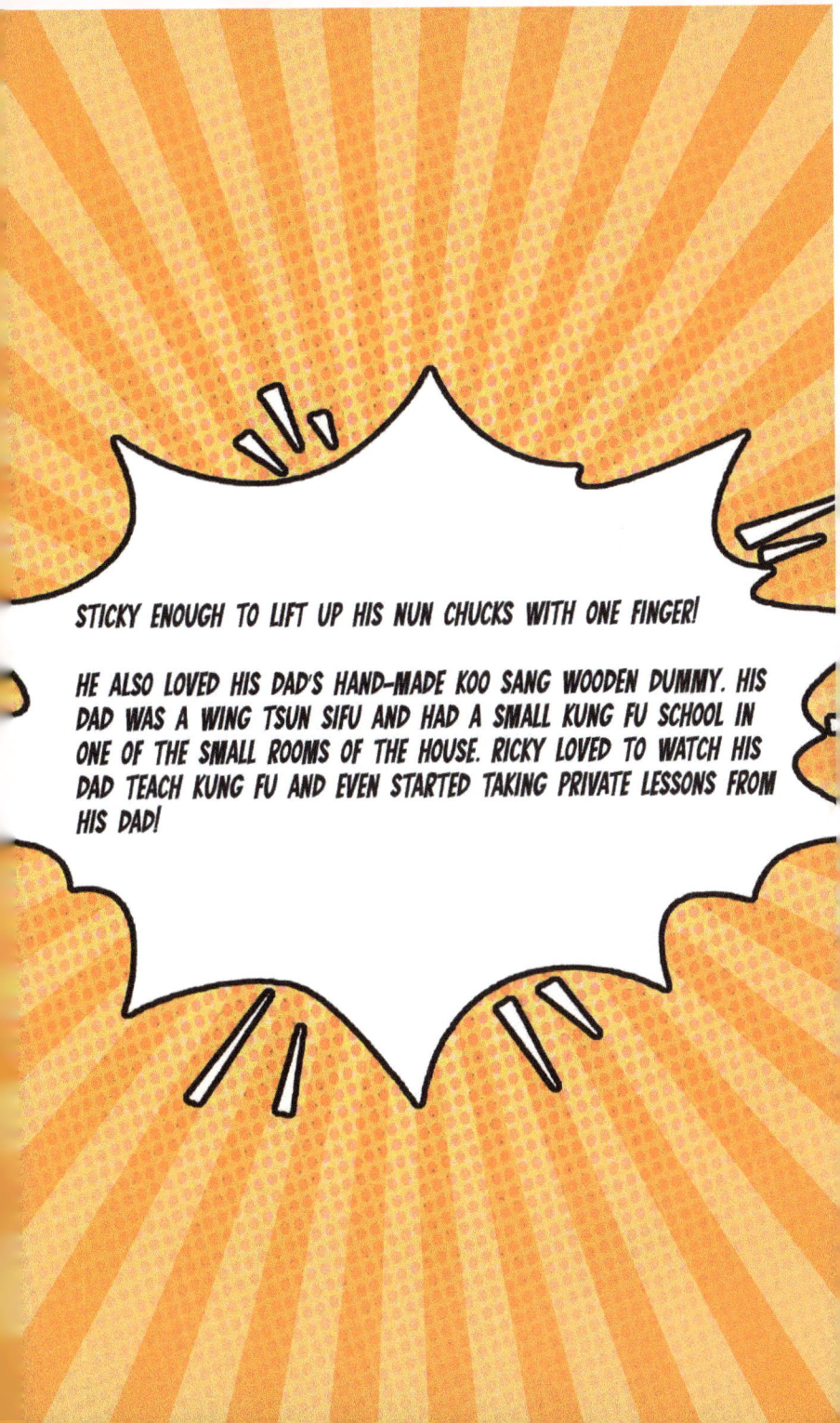

STICKY ENOUGH TO LIFT UP HIS NUN CHUCKS WITH ONE FINGER!

HE ALSO LOVED HIS DAD'S HAND-MADE KOO SANG WOODEN DUMMY. HIS DAD WAS A WING TSUN SIFU AND HAD A SMALL KUNG FU SCHOOL IN ONE OF THE SMALL ROOMS OF THE HOUSE. RICKY LOVED TO WATCH HIS DAD TEACH KUNG FU AND EVEN STARTED TAKING PRIVATE LESSONS FROM HIS DAD!

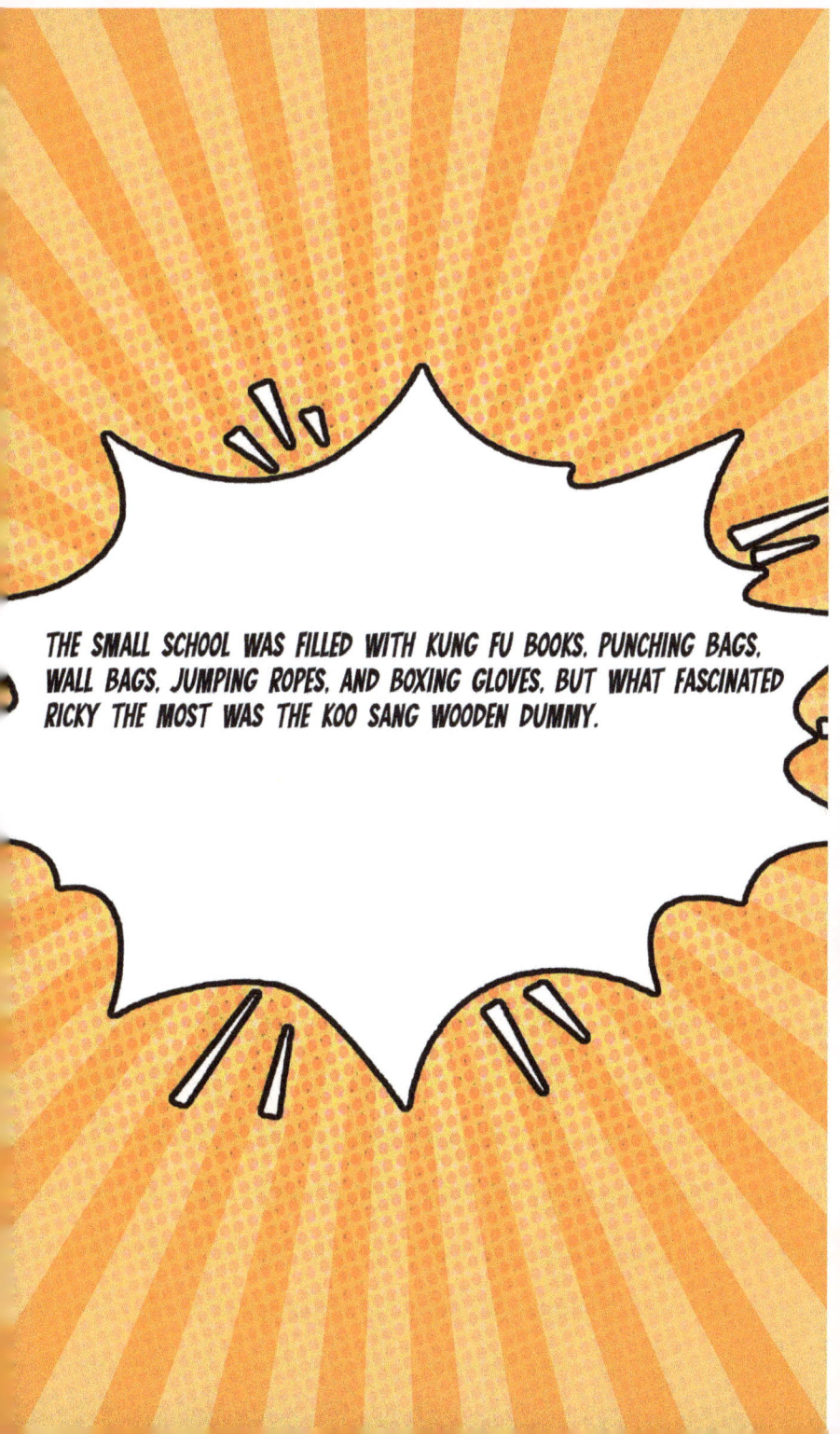

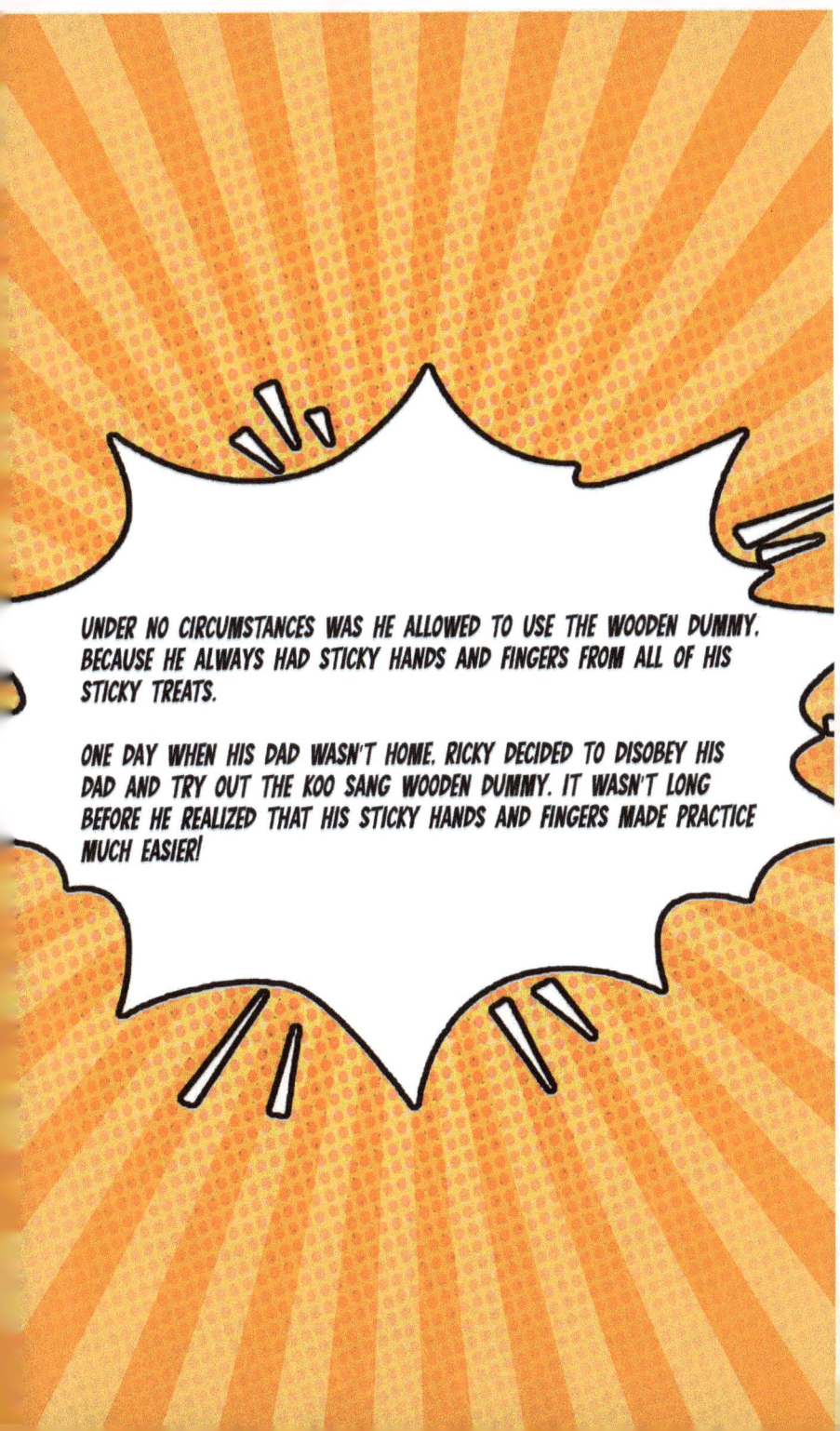

UNDER NO CIRCUMSTANCES WAS HE ALLOWED TO USE THE WOODEN DUMMY, BECAUSE HE ALWAYS HAD STICKY HANDS AND FINGERS FROM ALL OF HIS STICKY TREATS.

ONE DAY WHEN HIS DAD WASN'T HOME, RICKY DECIDED TO DISOBEY HIS DAD AND TRY OUT THE KOO SANG WOODEN DUMMY. IT WASN'T LONG BEFORE HE REALIZED THAT HIS STICKY HANDS AND FINGERS MADE PRACTICE MUCH EASIER!

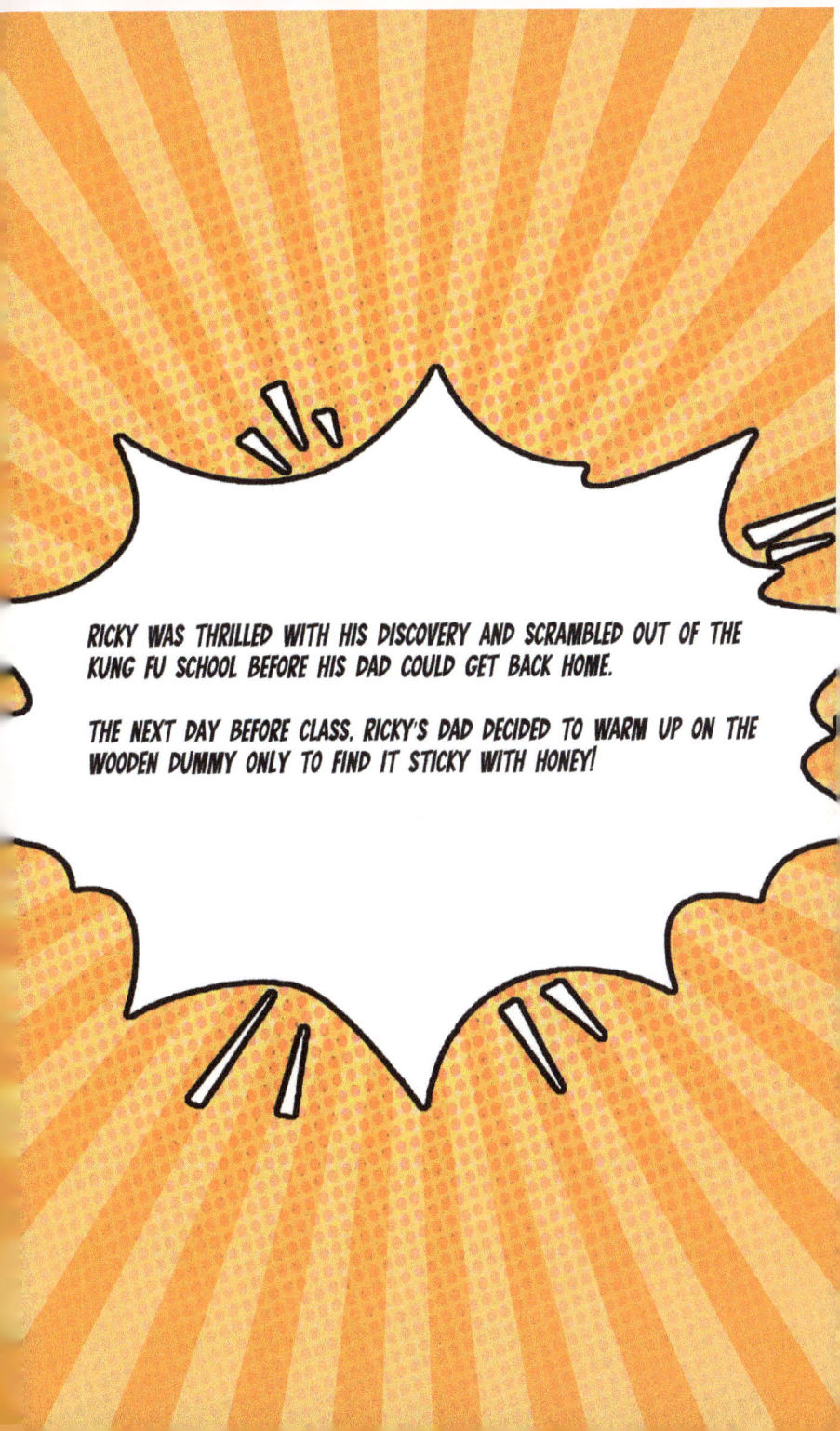

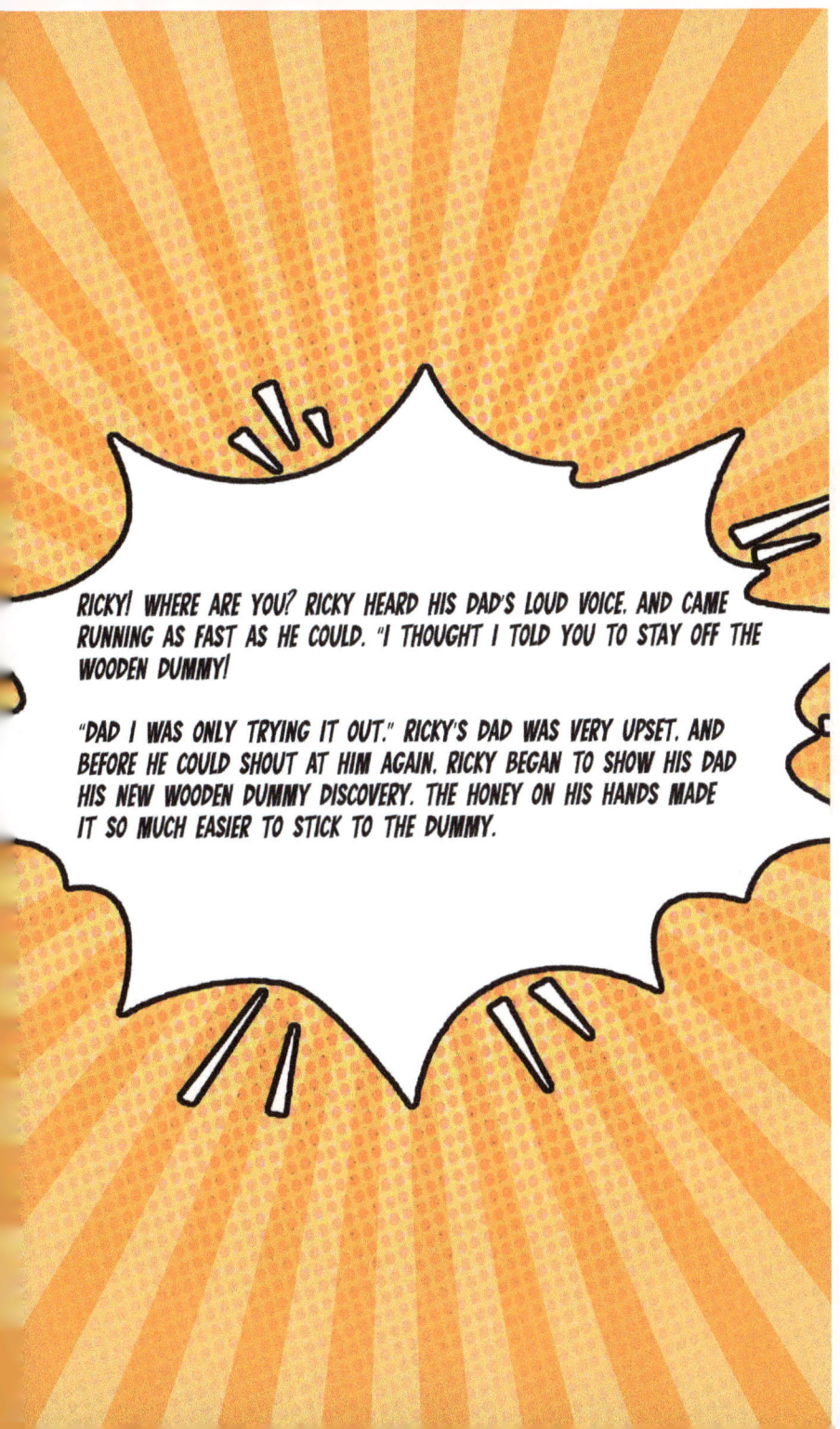

RICKY! WHERE ARE YOU? RICKY HEARD HIS DAD'S LOUD VOICE, AND CAME RUNNING AS FAST AS HE COULD. "I THOUGHT I TOLD YOU TO STAY OFF THE WOODEN DUMMY!

"DAD I WAS ONLY TRYING IT OUT." RICKY'S DAD WAS VERY UPSET, AND BEFORE HE COULD SHOUT AT HIM AGAIN, RICKY BEGAN TO SHOW HIS DAD HIS NEW WOODEN DUMMY DISCOVERY. THE HONEY ON HIS HANDS MADE IT SO MUCH EASIER TO STICK TO THE DUMMY.

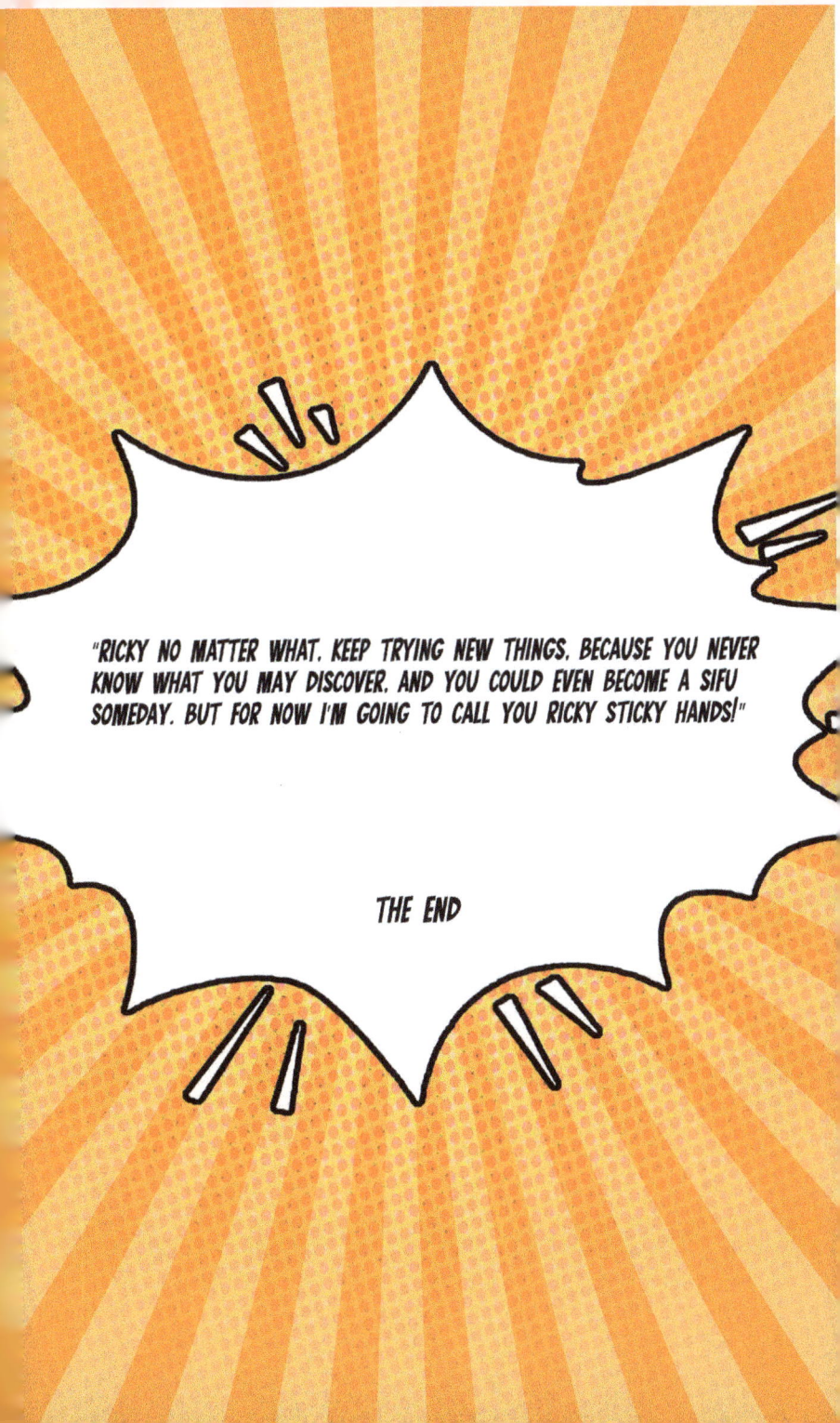

www.ingramcontent.com/pod-product-compliance
Lightning Source LLC
Chambersburg PA
CBHW061742070526
44585CB00024B/2783